The Tariff Idea

The Foundation for Economic Education, Inc.
Irvington-on-Hudson, New York

The Tariff Idea

The Foundation for Economic Education, Inc.
30 South Broadway
Irvington-on-Hudson, NY 10533
(914)591-7230

Publisher's Cataloging in Publication
(Prepared by Quality Books, Inc.)

Curtiss, W. M. (William Marshall), 1904–1979
    The tariff idea / W. M. Curtiss
    p. cm.
    Originally published 1953.
    ISBN 0-910614-46-6

    1. Tariff.   I. Title

HF1713.M37 1996   382.7
                          QBI96-20296

Library of Congress Catalog Card Number: 96-85396

Third printing, July 1996

Manufactured in the United States of America

Contents

The Tariff Idea

More than a century ago, Frederic Bastiat, a French economist and an ardent opponent of protectionism, drew on Daniel Defoe's immortal classic, *Robinson Crusoe,* to illustrate the evils of trade restrictions:

"You remember how Robinson Crusoe managed to make a plank when he had no saw."

"Yes; he felled a tree, and then, cutting the trunk right and left with his hatchet, he reduced it to the thickness of a board."

"And that cost him much labour?"

"Fifteen whole days' work."

"And what did he live on during that time?"

"He had provisions."

"What happened to the hatchet?"

"It was blunted by the work."

"Yes; but you perhaps do not know this: that at the moment when Robinson was beginning the work he perceived a plank thrown by the tide upon the seashore."

"Happy accident! He of course ran to appropriate it?"

"That was his first impulse; but he stopped short, and began to reason thus with himself:

" 'If I get this plank, it will cost me only the trouble of carrying it, and the time needed to descend and remount the cliff. But if I form a plank with my hatchet, first of all, it will procure me fifteen days' employment; then my hatchet will get blunt, which will furnish me with the additional employment of sharpening it; then I shall consume my stock of provisions, which will be a third source of employment in replacing them. Now, labour is wealth. It is clear that I should ruin myself by getting the plank. I must protect my personal labour; and, now that I think of it, I can even increase that labour by throwing back the plank into the sea.' "

Absurd Reasoning

"But this reasoning was absurd."

"No doubt. It is nevertheless the reasoning of every nation which protects itself by prohibition. It throws back the plank which is offered in exchange for a small amount of labour in order to exert a greater amount of labour. Even in the labour of the Custom-house officials it discovers a gain. That gain is represented by the pains which Robinson takes to render back to the waves the gift which they had offered him. Consider the nation as a collective being, and you will not find between its reasoning and that of Robinson an atom of difference."

8

"Did Robinson not see that he could devote the time saved to something else?"

"What else?"

"As long as a man has wants to satisfy and time at his disposal, there is always something to be done. I am not bound to specify the kind of labour he would in such a case undertake."

"I see clearly what labour he could have escaped."

"And I maintain that Robinson, with incredible blindness, confounded the labour with its result, the end with the means, and I am going to prove to you . . ."

"There is no need. Here we have the system of restriction or prohibition in its simplest form. If it appear to you absurd when so put, it is because the two capacities of producer and consumer are in this case mixed up in the same individual."

"Let us pass on, therefore, to a more complicated example."

"With all my heart. Some time afterwards, Robinson having met with Friday, they united their labour in a common work. In the morning they hunted for six hours, and brought home four baskets of game. In the evening they worked in the garden for six hours, and obtained four baskets of vegetables."

A Visiting Foreigner

"One day a canoe touched at the island. A good-looking foreigner landed, and was admitted to the

9

table of our two recluses. He tasted and commended very much the produce of the garden, and before taking leave of his entertainers, spoke as follows:

" 'Generous islanders, I inhabit a country where game is much more plentiful than here, but where horticulture is quite unknown. It would be an easy matter to bring you every evening four baskets of game, if you will give me in exchange two baskets of vegetables.'

"At these words Robinson and Friday retired to consult, and the debate that took place is too interesting not to be reported in extenso.

"Friday: What do you think of it?

"Robinson: If we close with the proposal, we are ruined.

"F: Are you sure of that? Let us consider.

"R: The case is clear. Crushed by competition, our hunting as a branch of industry is annihilated.

"F: What matters it, if we have the game?

"R: Theory! It will no longer be the product of our labour.

"F: I beg your pardon, sir; for in order to have game we must part with vegetables.

"R: Then, what shall we gain?

"F: The four baskets of game cost us six hours' work. The foreigner gives us them in exchange for two baskets of vegetables, which cost us only three hours' work. This places three hours at our disposal.

"R: Say, rather, which are subtracted from our exertions. There is our loss. Labour is wealth, and if we lose a fourth part of our time we shall be less rich by a fourth.

"F: You are greatly mistaken, my good friend. We shall have as much game, and the same quantity of vegetables, and three hours at our disposal into the bargain. This is progress, or there is no such thing in the world.

"R: You lose yourself in generalities! What should we make of these three hours?

"F: We would do something else.

"R: Ah! I understand you. You cannot come to particulars. Something else, something else—that is easily said.

Alternatives

"F: We can fish, we can ornament our cottage, we can read the Bible.

"R: Utopia! Is there any certainty that we should do either the one or the other?

"F: Very well, if we have no wants to satisfy we can rest. Is repose nothing?

"R: But while we repose we may die of hunger.

"F: My dear friend, you have got into a vicious circle. I speak of a repose which will subtract nothing from our supply of game and vegetables. You always forget that by means of our foreign trade nine hours' labour will give us the same quantity of provisions that we obtain at present with twelve.

"R: It is very evident, Friday, that you have not been educated in Europe, and that you have never read the Moniteur Industriel. If you had, it would have taught you this: that all time saved is sheer loss. The important thing is not to eat or consume, but to work. All that we consume, if it is not the direct produce of our labour, goes for nothing. Do you want to know whether you are rich? Never consider the enjoyments you obtain, but the labour you undergo. This is what the Moniteur Industriel would teach you. For myself, who have no pretensions to be a theorist, the only thing I look at is the loss of our hunting.

A Strange Idea

"F: What a strange turning upside down of ideas! But . . .

"R: No buts. Moreover, there are political reasons for rejecting the interested offers of the perfidious foreigner.

"F: Political reasons!

"R: Yes, he only makes us these offers because they are advantageous to him.

"F: So much the better, since they are for our advantage likewise.

"R: Then by this traffic we should place ourselves in a situation of dependence upon him.

"F: And he would place himself in dependence on us. We should have need of his game, and he of our vegetables, and we should live on terms of friendship.

"R: System! Do you want me to shut your mouth?

"F: We shall see about that. I have as yet heard no good reason.

"R: Suppose the foreigner learns to cultivate a garden, and that his island should prove more fertile than ours. Do you see the consequence?

"F: Yes; our relations with the foreigner would cease. He

would take from us no more vegetables, since he could have them at home with less labour. He would bring us no more game, since we should have nothing to give him in exchange, and we should then be in precisely the situation that you wish us in now.

Fears

"R: Improvident savage! You don't see that after having annihilated our hunting by inundating us with game, he would annihilate our gardening by inundating us with vegetables.

"F: But this would only last so long as we were in a situation to give him something else; that is to say, so long as we found something else which we could produce with economy of labour for ourselves.

"R: Something else, something else! You always come back to that. You are at sea, my good friend Friday; there is nothing practical in your views.

"The debate was long prolonged, and, as often happens, each remained wedded to his own opinion. But Robinson possessing a great influence over Friday, his opinion prevailed, and when the foreigner arrived to demand a reply, Robinson said to him:

" 'Stranger, in order to induce us to accept your proposal, we must be assured of two things: The first is, that your island is no better stocked with game than ours, for we want to fight only with equal weapons. The second is that you will lose by the bargain. For, as in every exchange there is necessarily a gaining and a losing party, we should be dupes, if you were not the loser. What have you got to say?'

" 'Nothing,' replied the foreigner; and, bursting out laughing, he regained his canoe."*

A Present-day Need

Bastiat's keen analysis of what he called "protectionism" is as much needed today as it was then. Contained in his skillful amplification of *Robinson Crusoe* are simple illustrations of most of the arguments for and against tariffs that have been and are still being used by the leaders, political and otherwise, of every nation.

Tariffs are only one of the many restrictions to trade throughout the world. For many years, they were perhaps the most important restriction; but more recently, their importance has been overshadowed by such modern innovations as exchange controls, quotas on imports and exports, bilateral and multilateral agreements, most-favored-nation agreements, bulk buying and selling by nations, fair trade laws, subsidies, national and international give-away programs, and so on.

Tariffs are discussed here, not because of their current importance relative to other restrictions, but because they have persisted so long in the face of well-reasoned opposition. It is probable that if the effects of tariffs were

*Frederic Bastiat, *Social Fallacies* (Santa Ana, Calif.: Register Publishing Co., Ltd., 1944), pp. 202-6. Translated by Patrick James Stirling. (First published in the *Journal des Economistes*, France, 1844.) Further quotations from Bastiat throughout this study are from the same book.

clearly understood, a better understanding of the various other trade restrictions might evolve because the same basic fallacies seem to underlie them all. Tariffs are a form of price control. One who defends tariffs cannot logically oppose government control of prices and profits, material allocations, subsidies, and other violations of the free-market principle.

Agreement among Economists

Professional economists have long been accused of being unable to agree on the causes and solutions of major economic problems. However true that accusation may be, here is a problem on which economists have been in substantial agreement for 200 years or more. Textbooks, modern and not-so-modern, have pointed out repeatedly the harmful effects of tariffs on the well-being of individuals the world over.

In his widely used college textbook, *Economic Analysis,* Professor Kenneth E. Boulding says:

"In the face of a hundred and fifty years of denunciation by the economists, tariffs continue to grow. In view of the almost universal rejection of his advice by practical politicians and business men, the economist perhaps has a duty to explain not only why the policies which he advocates are right but why they are unpopular. The explanation follows two lines. The first is political rather than economic. Governments, even democratic governments, tend to be swayed by noisy minorities rather than by silent majorities. Any particular tariff, in the short run—which is all practical people ever care about—will benefit a particular industry. This industry is relatively small, usually well organized, acutely conscious of its possible gains, and vocal. The tariff will injure all the rest of us. But everybody is nobody. The rest of us are diffuse, unorganized, unconscious of our common interest, and silent. It is small wonder that we are so little regarded."*

Why is it, then, that tariffs persist? Is it because they are a political issue? Is it because the imposing of tariffs is subject to pressure-group action by strong minorities? Or is it, perhaps, because we who are most affected by tariffs do not understand them and thus do not look after our own interests?

Tariffs and Political Parties

There can be no doubt that at times tariffs have been associated with politics. At one time, the question of tariffs was considered to be the major point of difference between the two great political parties of this nation. One was called the "high tariff" party and the other the "low tariff" party. But today if you were to ask the younger voters of the nation which party was which, it is doubtful whether many could answer correctly.

In economic problems as well as in all others, truth—once it is widely recognized—will prevail. And once

---

*Kenneth E. Boulding, *Economic Analysis* (New York: Harper & Brothers, 1941), p. 347.

there is sufficient understanding of tariffs, this restriction to trade will be eliminated.

Let us approach the study of tariffs with the assumption that protectionists have a sincere belief in tariffs, not simply a selfish interest. As Bastiat said: "The doctrine of protection is too popular not to be sincere." If this be true—and I believe it is for the most part—then a convincing explanation of the fallacy of the tariff idea will permanently remove that particular restriction against trade.

In preparation for a consideration of the tariff problem, let us discuss seven basic assumptions to which practically everyone will agree. It may seem unnecessary to do this since these assumptions are so generally accepted; but the advocates of tariffs, while perhaps agreeing to these assumptions, often violate them in their defense of tariffs and other trade restrictions.

1. The Right to Own Property

Ask any cross section of people in this country if they believe in an individual's right to own property, and an overwhelming majority will say: "Why, of course!" This belief is so commonly accepted as a part of our way of life that it is seldom questioned. Yet in actual practice, the principle underlying the belief is constantly violated.

The free exchange of goods and services between individuals depends on the idea that a person has the right to own property. If a person has the right to own

17

property, it follows that he has the right to use or dispose of his property as he wishes, so long as he does not infringe on the same right of others.*

2. Doing Things the Easy Way

Man attempts to satisfy his desires with the least possible effort—a worthy trait indeed, so long as he does not tread on the equal right of others to do the same. This is the *principle of conservation* as applied to human effort—and it is the basis of all progress.

In satisfying his desires, modern man is constantly exchanging goods and services with other men. In making these exchanges, his urge is always to obtain something which he values more highly than what he gives up.

A certain primitive man may have discovered that he was very clever at catching small game and that at the end of the day he had more than enough for his family's needs. But he was a terrible fisherman, and after fishing all day he had little to show for his efforts. His neighbor may have been an able fisherman but a poor hunter. So the one who was poor at fishing discovered that he could trade half a day's hunt for many more fish than he could catch in half a day. A trade was made, and both men benefited. This may have been the beginning of the Age of Specialization—man simply trying to satisfy his desires with the least possible effort.

---

*For a more complete discussion of this subject, see: F. A. Harper, *Gaining the Free Market* (Irvington-on-Hudson, N. Y.: Foundation for Economic Education, Inc., 1952).

But this trait in man's nature sometimes leads to trouble. Some men think that the easiest way to satisfy their wants is to steal from others. And perhaps this would be so except for one thing: The victims resent it. In most societies, of course, stealing is considered to be a violation of the basic codes of conduct, ethics, and morality; it is a violation of our first assumption, *a person has the right to own property*. If stealing is considered wrong in a society, it is natural that laws be passed to punish thieves.

Legalized Theft

Through the years, some men have discovered how to satisfy their wants at the expense of others without being accused of theft: They ask their government to do the stealing for them.

This method of trying to get something for nothing has spread all over the world in recent years. It is simply a perverted expression of man's laziness—of his desire to satisfy his wants with the least possible effort on his part.

Most people tend to forget the moral arguments against stealing; they forget the basis of morality and look to statutory law as the guide. This is the way in which men have come to use government to pervert the law into an instrument of the tyranny it was designed to suppress. The solution requires a restatement of the code of ethics and a reapplication of the moral codes long known by men.

3. Scarcity versus Abundance

The material welfare of an individual, a family, a group, or a nation is determined by the amount of goods and services at its disposal. A nation, like an individual, cannot consume what it does not have. Thus, the material level of living which the people of a nation enjoy is measured by their production—plus or minus international gifts.

The American family has more material things than has the Chinese or Indian or Russian family because the American worker produces more. The reasons for this greater productivity—capital accumulation, private ownership, tools, etc.—are fairly well known and are not a part of this story. The point we are trying to establish here is that high-level consumption is based on high-level production and exchange—on abundance, not on scarcity.

True enough, the scarcity theory of economics has been and is being advocated in America and elsewhere. The difficulty seems to arise when *money* is confused with *things*. As producers, some groups discover that by making an article scarce they can increase its price. This is, of course, true; and the idea is embodied in all sorts of schemes to curb production—featherbedding, licensing all kinds of business, limiting the hours of work and the number of bricks a mason may lay in a day, restricting the width of paint brushes, maintaining the number of firemen on a diesel locomotive, and so on and on. Not long ago, we were told that this nation could become richer by destroying some of its real wealth—by such tactics as plowing under part of its cotton crop and destroying some of its pigs.

Also, each individual producer observes that if all others producing the same thing would limit their output, he could get a higher price for his product. But looking at production from the consumer's standpoint, hardly anyone will deny that an abundance of the things people want is what makes possible a high level of living. Bastiat put it this way:

"The consumer is richer in proportion as he purchases all things cheaper; and he purchases things cheaper in proportion to their abundance; therefore it is abundance which enriches him. This reasoning, extended to all consumers, leads to the theory of plenty . . . . As sellers we have an interest in dearness, and consequently in scarcity; as buyers, in cheapness, or what amounts to the same thing, in the abundance of commodities . . . .

"If man were a solitary animal, if he laboured exclusively for himself, if he consumed directly the fruit of his labour—in a word, if he did not exchange—the theory of scarcity would never have appeared in the world . . . . No solitary man would ever have thought that in order to encourage his labour and render it more productive, it was necessary to break in pieces the instruments which saved it, to neutralize the fertility of the soil, or give back to the sea the good things it had brought to his door. He would perceive at once that labour is not an end, but a means."

4. Who Profits from Free Exchange?

When two men voluntarily agree to trade horses, it is certain that each believes he is to get something better than what he is to give up. Why else would either consent to the trade? This is so obvious that it should not be necessary to defend it.

When exchange becomes more complicated—when money is traded for goods or services, or when there is a three-way exchange—we sometimes lose sight of the fact that all parties involved consider themselves benefited by the exchange, if it is *voluntary*.

There seems to be a general feeling that when money is exchanged for, say, an automobile, it is only the seller of the car who benefits. But doesn't the buyer benefit as well? Doesn't he value the car more than the money he gives up? If not, why does he willingly make the exchange?

Is it any different when the bargaining parties happen to live in different cities? Or in different states? Or in different countries? If an importer in New York voluntarily gives up dollars to a British exporter of woolens, who is to say which party benefits?—and by how much? Unless each thinks he will be better off by reason of the exchange, why does he agree to it?

One might argue that England, as a whole, would be better off if she kept her woolens, and we, our dollars. As a matter of fact, such is the assumption of government officials all over the world when they establish trade restrictions—tariffs, export quotas, exchange controls, and other trade barriers. Such officials, denying that these decisions should be made by the parties concerned, have substituted their own judgments of the advantage or disadvantage of an exchange. It would be just as logical for the government to step in and regulate the trading by two small boys of a baseball for a jackknife. After all, someone "in all his wisdom" may honestly believe that Johnny would be better off if he kept his baseball than if he traded it for a knife.

There are many people in the world today who hold that individuals are incapable of determining their own best interests. They will maintain, if they are consistent, that voluntary exchange of goods or services between individuals cannot be relied on to benefit the group as a whole. Such a belief is refuted by 150 years of progress under a fairly free exchange system within this country.

5. The Age of Specialization

The present century is often referred to as the Age of Specialization. This is true to a degree. But any era in recorded history could have been, and probably was, called an Age of Specialization. There is little doubt that even among primitive men there were individuals who developed special skills which improved the productivity of their efforts.

With the development of these skills, exchange became advantageous. The tribesman who was especially clever at fashioning arrowheads from pieces of flint may have traded his arrows to advantage with someone more skillful than he in hunting or fishing or something else.

So throughout history, and to a dramatic degree in the past 100 years, men have become specialists. Suppose, for instance, that each person had to produce his own television set. Life just wouldn't be long enough for him to do it. He would have to be an electronics engineer, a mining engineer, a metallurgist, a cabinetmaker, a glass manufacturer, a machine-tool maker—there must be hundreds of skills involved in building a television set.

But while he was mastering the skills necessary to produce his television set, who would provide him with food, clothing, and shelter? And how could he learn electronics without books and the accumulation of years of research?

Not many decades past, practically every working hour was required just to provide the food, clothing, and shelter necessary to keep alive. Most people were farmers. There was precious little besides the products of the farm available to families, for the simple reason that eight or nine out of every ten families had to work as hard as they could to feed and clothe the ten families. Specialization? Yes, they had it in a limited way. But today in the United States, it requires little more than one family in ten to produce enough food and animal fiber for all ten families. The other nine families can make television sets, automobiles, household furnishings; they can be teachers, doctors, clergymen, or producers of a host of other goods and services.

Specialization is made possible by what economists call "comparative advantage." We see this clearly in athletic events. Some persons are better than others at throwing a ball or batting a ball or passing a football or playing tennis or running or jumping. They have a comparative advantage and thus are specialists. The same is true of writing a novel, operating a typewriter or a punch press, or treating a disease.

Expensive Bananas

Comparative advantage is sometimes the result of geography. A clear example is the production of bananas. Bananas can be grown under glass in the state of New York—and a few are. Of course, they are very expensive when grown this way. Through the co-operation of nature, bananas are grown at much less cost in Central America. That area, then, has a comparative advantage in the growing of bananas.

Another example, not quite so obvious, is the raising of beef cattle. They are raised in New York State in a limited way; but with the opening of the ranges in the West and of the feed lots in the corn belt, the raising of beef cattle ceased to be a major enterprise in New York —not because they can't be grown in New York, but rather because they can be grown to better advantage elsewhere. New York farmers now find an advantage in specializing in the production of milk, poultry, fruit, and vegetables.

So it is with nations. Conceivably, individuals within one nation might be highly efficient at producing every single thing wanted by the people of that nation. Still, by trading with people in other nations, they direct their own productive efforts toward those things which they can produce to *greatest* advantage. Cost of production is not a complete guide to what will be produced, unless one includes in the cost of production what economists call "opportunity costs."

Thus, the principle of comparative advantage is constantly at work all over the world. It operates not only between nations, but also between parts of the same nation—from town to town, from farm to farm, and even from individual to individual.

6. What Makes Wages High?

In a free, competitive market, the price of a commodity or service depends on what someone is willing to pay for it. So it is with the wages of labor. The employer must be willing to pay if he wants men to work for him. How much he will pay will depend, in turn, on how much his workers can produce.

Therefore, we find relatively high wages in a country where the productivity of the workers is high. Where we find an extremely low level of wages, we can be sure that the productivity of the workers is low. Here, of course, we are speaking of *real* wages—what the wages will purchase—rather than of *money* wages. In a country experiencing great inflation, money wages may climb to astronomical heights and yet buy very little.

Why there is such a tremendous difference in the production of workers in different countries is not really a part of this story, but it can be summed up very briefly in the one word, *tools*. The term *tools* includes plant and equipment, as well as the actual machines the worker operates. A man who has good tools with which to work is more productive than one who has poor tools. In the United States, it now requires an average investment of $16,600 to provide one industrial worker with tools. A new steel plant recently built on the Delaware River is reported to have cost $90,000 for each worker who will be employed there.

To provide the tools for the workers, a part of the past production of individuals must be saved. There is no other way. Workers compete with one another for the use of tools; the more plentiful the supply of tools, the better each worker's chance of being highly paid for using them. Workers who use their organized power to frustrate production, thus preventing the saving for new tools—new capital—tend to cut off their only avenue to progress.

7. Consumption the Purpose of Production

In an economic sense, the only reason for producing anything is to satisfy the desires of consumers. This idea seems simple enough, but it is often lost from sight as an economy becomes more and more complex and specialized.

In a subsistence economy, where the producer is also the consumer, production is obviously for consumption. In such an economy, the family is acutely aware that it must produce food in order to eat; to provide its clothing, sheep must be raised or fur-bearing animals hunted. The family is both producer and consumer of everything it has.

Despite Bastiat's satire on Robinson Crusoe, it is unthinkable that Crusoe would have hesitated to take the plank washed in by the waves, thus saving himself the labor of hewing one from a log.

Nowadays, with our high degree of specialization, production and consumption may be widely separated. For example, a worker may have a small part in producing the steel which will eventually be used to make a watch spring. But his wages are in money, not in steel or watches. While he may be a consumer of watches through a roundabout exchange process, he may overlook the fact that what he helps to produce determines what he may consume.

The Mercantile System

Adam Smith explained the relation between production and consumption nearly 200 years ago. In his *The Wealth of Nations,* published in the year of the signing of our Declaration of Independence, Smith said:

"Consumption is the sole end and purpose of all production; and the interest of the producer ought to be attended to, only so far as it may be necessary for promoting that of the consumer. The maxim is so perfectly self-evident, that it would be absurd to attempt to prove it. But in the mercantile system, the interest of the consumer is almost constantly sacrificed to that of the producer; and it seems to consider production, and not consumption, as the ultimate end and object of all industry and commerce."*

In his discussion of tariffs, Bastiat compares trade with a horse race. He begins by quoting the statement of M. le Vicomte de Romanet, a fellow Frenchman:

"It has been thought that protection in our case should simply represent the difference which exists between the cost price of a commodity which we produce and the cost price of the same commodity produced by our neighbors. . . . A protective duty calculated on this basis would only ensure free competition. . . ; free competition exists only when there is equality in the conditions and in the charges. In the case of a horse-race, we ascertain the weight which each horse has to carry, and so equalise the conditions; without that there could be no fair competition. In the case of trade, if one of the sellers can bring his commodity to market at less cost, he ceases to be a competitor, and becomes a monopolist. . . . Do away with this protection which represents the difference of cost price, and the foreigner invades our markets and acquires a monopoly."

This says, in effect, that competition is not present if any competitor wins by his efficiency. Bastiat replies:

*Smith was speaking of the mercantilists' point of view, which was that exports were to be promoted while domestic production was "safeguarded" against competing imports. Adam Smith, *The Wealth of Nations* (Modern Library ed.; New York: Random House, Inc., 1937), p. 625.

"In this, as in other cases, we shall find protectionist theorists viewing their subject from the producer's standpoint, whilst we advocate the cause of the unfortunate consumers, whose interests they studiously keep out of sight. . . . The race is at once the means and the end. . . . When you start your horses, your end, your object, is to find out which is the swiftest runner, and I see your reason for equalising the weights. But if your end, your object, were to secure the arrival of some important and urgent news at the winning-post, could you, without inconsistency, throw obstacles in the way of anyone who should offer you the best means of expediting your message?"

The *end* with which Bastiat was concerned was consumption—not production, which is merely a *means* to that end.

Using Romanet's reasoning, we would place a very high tariff on bananas. Suppose, for example, that the cost of raising hothouse bananas in New York is one dollar a pound and that they can be imported from Central America for ten cents a pound. A tariff of 90 cents a pound would then insure "fair" competition between New York and Central American producers.

On this basis, it is probably true that the New York producer would stay in business and grow bananas. But what of the consumer? What price would he have to pay for bananas? What would happen to the consumption of bananas? And while the New Yorker was producing high-priced bananas, might he not have been producing something else that would yield many times the amount of satisfaction to the consumers—and to himself as one of those consumers?

A Further Application

The same reasoning could be applied to the production of cotton, wheat, beef cattle, and hogs on New York farms. Tariffs could be raised at New York's borders to permit "free" competition—as Romanet thought of it—with other areas in the United States which have a comparative advantage in the production of these things. If the reasoning applies between nations, it surely applies between states, between counties, and even between neighboring farms. If followed to its logical conclusion, this reasoning would demand a completely self-sufficient economy for each family or for each person.

Many of the economic fallacies which abound today stem from a failure to see that consumption is the sole purpose of production. The "labor theory of value" is one such fallacy. This theory, which states that the value of a thing depends upon the amount of work required to produce it, was modified somewhat by Karl Marx in his "surplus value" theory. Under the labor theory of value, the plank hewed from a log by Crusoe would be of much greater value than the plank washed up by the waves.

The labor theory of value is now known to be inconsistent with the basic principles of an exchange economy. Voluntary exchange depends upon the acceptance of the "market theory of value." According to this theory, the value of an article depends upon what the consumer will pay for it *voluntarily*. The highest bidder, of course, may be the producer himself, in which case there will be no exchange; but that is one of the desirable alternatives which freedom of choice affords.

The Consumer Is King

The market theory of value recognizes the consumer as king—as the guide for all production. By this test, the two equally good planks which Crusoe was considering would have been worth the same to him; he would have chosen the one which cost him the least in time and effort.

In a free market, the consumer has no *direct* concern with the cost of production. He merely looks over the alternatives presented in the market and bids what he is willing to give for what he wants. No matter how complex the market appears to be, it is simply the place where the available supply and the current demand are equated through price.

The consumer is, in effect, the court of last appeal in a free market. He is the judge who convicts or acquits. He either accepts or rejects the goods and services offered—taking into account his own desires, his buying power, and the alternate products available. He cares not a whit, at the moment, what it may have cost someone to produce the goods.

To ignore these decisions of the consumer is economic suicide—witness the demise each year of business firms which were guilty of ignoring or misjudging the consumer.

Apparently many persons have lost sight of the fact that consumption is the sole purpose of production. This is indicated by the prevalent belief that production is sometimes for *profit* rather than for *use*—the assumption being that a producer can fix the price of what he produces at any level, ignoring the wishes of the consumer. When a producer, laboring under this false assumption, enters the free market with his product, he will soon find, much to his sorrow, that the consumer is actually king. Unless he serves the consumer well and efficiently, his hoped-for profit will prove to be only a mirage. In a free market, all economic production is for use—as judged by the consumer; it cannot possibly be otherwise. If a suitable profit is realized by the producer, he is happy and will probably continue to serve the king—the consumer.

Thus, we have briefly discussed seven assumptions which will serve as a basis for discussing tariffs:

1. Man has a basic right to own and to exchange property.
2. Man seeks to satisfy his desires with the least possible effort.
3. Scarcity is not a means to better living.
4. Free, voluntary exchange occurs because all parties see a chance to gain.
5. Specialization is a key to progress.
6. High wages result from high productivity through better tools—capital.
7. Consumption is the sole purpose of production.

It will be recognized at once that these basic assumptions are useful in considering many current economic questions besides tariffs. We shall use them, however, primarily in considering some of the arguments used in defense of tariffs and other types of trade restriction.

Tariffs for Revenue

Tariffs are commonly classified into two groups— those for *protection* and those for *revenue*. Actually, of course, no such exclusive classification can logically be made. If the tariff is so high that it completely prevents a potential import from coming into the country, it is entirely for the "protection" of the domestic producer, and no revenue results. If the tariff is low enough to allow imports to come in, it produces some revenue; but at the same time, it continues to partially "protect" the domestic producer. This "protection" continues as long as there is any tariff at all.

The only way a tariff could possibly serve *only* for revenue would be to apply it to an import which is not and will not be produced in this country. But even in that situation, American consumers would pay more for this product than they would if there were no tariff— thus reducing the amount of money available for expenditure in other ways.

In the early days of our nation's history, tariffs were an important source of revenue because this was the principal device used by the federal government to raise its funds. The first bill passed by the first Congress was a tariff act. In the decade from 1800 to 1810, customs receipts constituted 92 per cent of the income of the national government.

The Sixteenth Amendment

Since the advent of the federal income tax, made possible by the Sixteenth Amendment in 1913, tariffs as a source of revenue have faded into insignificance. In the five years preceding World War II, customs receipts constituted only about 7 per cent of the total revenue; in more recent years, the percentage has declined to about 1 per cent. This remarkable decline in the proportion of federal income collected through tariffs is not, of course, the result of a general lowering of tariff rates since 1800. It is, rather, the result of the federal government's adding other sources of revenue. In 1800, the federal government took, in taxes, only one to two cents of each individual's income dollar; it now takes about 25 cents out of each dollar.

In trying to appraise a tariff which is levied for revenue purposes on a particular commodity, the same tests should be applied as are used to appraise an excise tax. In fact, a tariff in this sense should properly be called an excise tax.

The question of tariffs as a source of government revenue—as a tax—need not concern us here. But it should be remembered that tariffs have sometimes been imposed under the guise of being strictly for revenue purposes, whereas they were actually for purposes of protection.

Tariffs and the Balance of Trade

One of the fallacies popular throughout the world is the belief that exports are good and imports are bad. If we sell more than we buy, we have a "favorable" balance of trade—and that is supposed to be good. Actually, in a free market there is no such thing as a favorable or unfavorable balance of trade. There is simply a balance.

Trade between nations is not different in this respect from trade between individuals. Suppose you sell a bushel of apples for two dollars. You get two dollars, which you would rather have than the apples; the buyer gets the apples, which he would rather have than two dollars. A perfect balance!

True enough, our exporters may sell goods to English buyers and get sterling exchange. They may spend this money in France or Germany rather than in England, so that the flow of goods is not directly between England and America. But the same might be true in the trade of apples for dollars. With your two dollars, you probably will buy something from a third party rather than from the man who bought your apples.

If we are to buy, we must sell. If we are to export, we must import. It is just that simple. Erecting barriers against imports is just another way of cutting down our exports. There will still be a balance, but at a lower level.

Actually, tariffs have nothing to do with the balance of trade; they change the amount of trade, but the balance is still there. The optimum amount of foreign trade for any nation is that amount which will occur voluntarily when there are no artificial barriers to trade. It must be kept in mind that the term *trade* as used here refers to all exchanges—including services or travel or money or other types of "invisible" trade, as well as goods. The term refers to *economic* balance, rather than to *physical* balance.

Tariffs for Retaliation

When governments use tariffs and other trade restrictions as instruments to influence, restrain, or coerce other peoples or governments, the field of international politics and intrigue is entered. If history offers any basis for judgment on this subject, it is that sound economics and morality are cast aside at such times. This subject will be discussed more fully later, in connection with national defense.

International politicians seem to assume that trade is a hostile process; that it is a concession granted to friendly nations; and that when it is withheld from unfriendly nations it does them harm, without harming the withholder. Even the words sometimes used—*protection, sanction, embargo,* and the like—suggest hostility. They carry the implication of warfare—of doing something to restrain someone.

Actually, trade as engaged in by individuals is generally a friendly exchange. A trader, to be sure, drives the best bargain he can. But when both sides are free to accept or reject offers, the result cannot be hostile to either party. If you're out of gas, you don't feel hostile toward the person who sells you some.

In Bastiat's story of Robinson Crusoe and the stranger with game to be exchanged for vegetables, you will recall that Crusoe closed the conference by saying:

> "Stranger, in order to induce us to accept your proposal, we must be assured . . . that you will lose by the bargain. For, as in every exchange there is necessarily a gaining and a losing party, we should be dupes, if you were not the loser."

This attitude toward trade persists in the world today. It seems especially prevalent among government officials who wish to guide the world's business.

Most Favored Nation

In discussions of foreign trade, the term *most-favored-nation clause* is often used. This clause has, for several decades, been a part of many commercial treaties between nations. Its purpose is to prevent one nation's being treated more favorably than any other nation signing the commercial pact. Thus, no favoritism among the signatory nations. Back of this idea is the concept that by reducing tariffs we are granting a favor to the other nation. We are; but it would be more nearly correct to say that the most favored nation in every such deal is the one granting the reduction. Why is it a sacrificial act to grant a favor in which you yourself will share?

In the great expansion of trade restrictions following

World War I, some were imposed with the intent of retaliation. If country A raises a tariff wall against products from the United States, we are hurt by it; there's no doubt about that. Country A, however, may fail to realize that its citizens are hurt to an equal or an even greater degree. So, what do we do about it? We are likely to say: "You can't do this to us!" To drive home our conviction, we raise a retaliatory tariff against the products of country A. And who is affected by it? Country A, to be sure, is hurt by our tariff because its people will have greater difficulty in exporting goods to us over the tariff wall; but we, too, are hurt by our tariff against the other country's goods. Our consumers must pay more for imported goods which were formerly brought in duty-free. So the effect of such a combination of tariffs is to impoverish both nations. As Bastiat put it: "A protective duty is a tax directed against a foreign product; but we must never forget that it falls back on the home consumer."

Fight Fire with Fire

The view is commonly held that in a world of widespread economic nationalism, where nations have raised tariff walls against other nations, our only hope of survival is to do likewise. We must meet tariffs with tariffs —fight fire with fire. Such, of course, is not the case. Even if every single nation in the world raised tariffs against our products, we would gain in at least two ways by leaving our own borders open for the importation of goods. First, as consumers, we would benefit by the importation of goods and services shipped in at costs below those for which we could produce them. Second—and perhaps more important—this gesture would do more to establish friendly relations between nations than any other single thing we might do. Other nations would soon observe the wisdom of such a move and follow our example.

State Monopolies

In a similar vein, since many of the products we import are handled in the countries of origin by state monopolies, it is often argued that our government should serve as a monopoly in trade negotiations with those countries. This is specious reasoning at its worst. If a foreign government has control of all the tin production of its country and wants to sell this tin in the United States, is there any reason at all why it cannot deal directly with those Americans who want to buy tin? In this instance, the foreign government—if it will bargain in the market place—is just another individual so far as any buyer of tin is concerned. The amount of business involved in a trade—the "bigness" of the traders—does not alter the fact that each party seeks to get something of more value than that which he offers in exchange. When private individuals or firms of different countries deal with each other, there is little likelihood of their causing international incidents or unpleasantness; but when governments engage in business with each other, there is always the possibility of intrigue and violation of "national honor."

Do Tariffs Keep Wages High?

Probably the most common argument in defense of tariffs is that they keep our domestic wages high; that they keep wages in this country from being reduced to the level of wages in the countries from which we import. It is often put this way: "Tariffs protect us against the competition of low-paid foreign labor. If we accept their goods, we must accept their wage levels."

To begin with, we must not lose sight of the reason why wages in this country are higher than in some others. The level of wages depends upon the productivity of the workers. Our workers are highly productive, largely because of the tools with which they work. In countries where there is a limited accumulation of capital, the tools of the workers are limited. Thus their productivity is low, and the result is low wages.

The level of living in a nation depends upon the amount of goods and services available for consumption. If certain individuals in a nation voluntarily trade some of their possessions for the products of another country, it follows that what they receive is worth more to them than what they give up. Otherwise, they would not trade. The total value of the goods and services available for consumption is greater after the trade. The level of living has been raised.

Consider, for a moment, a product made entirely by

hand labor. Hand embroidery or other needlework will illustrate. Assume that a woman in Italy working for a very low wage can turn out handmade needlework comparable to that produced by an American woman working for a relatively high wage. It is obvious that the Italian product can be sold in this country cheaper than the American product. Does that mean that if we import the Italian product the American woman's wage will necessarily be reduced to the level of the Italian woman's wage? Not at all. Why is the wage of the American woman high? It is because of the generally high productivity of American labor, which makes it possible for her to get a high wage in an industrial plant, in an office, in a profession, or in some other type of employment.

It is true that, without trade barriers, hand embroidery might be imported from Italy. The American producer of hand embroidery, unable to produce and sell a comparable product at a competitive price, would have to turn to producing one of the many products for which he has a comparative advantage. The American producer might, for example, turn to machine production of embroidery.

A Necessary Readjustment

It is also true that the American woman who was doing hand embroidery would have to turn to some other employment. This is typical of the readjustments which would be necessitated by a return to free trade. Workers and management alike, having become adjusted to production under tariffs, would have to improve their efficiency or find other outlets for their skills.

The production of hand embroidery behind tariff walls in this country necessitates a higher price for the product. With the removal of the tariff, the price would drop, more embroidery would be sold and the former producers of hand embroidery in this country would turn to the production of something for which they have a greater comparative advantage. In the long run, everyone would gain from the abolition of the tariff on embroidery—including the American woman, who would find a better use for her time. and the Italian woman, who would find a greater outlet for her product.

Suppose a physician earning $10,000 a year buys his vegetables from a local farmer whose income is around $3,000. Does that mean that the doctor's income will decline toward that of the farmer? On the contrary! Both are specialists. By having someone else raise his vegetables, the doctor can specialize and become even more proficient in his job. If he were forced to raise his own vegetables and if the farmer were forced to doctor himself, neither would be as well off. Specialization and free trade improve the conditions of all participants. This is as true for foreign trade as for domestic trade.

Tariffs encourage the production of some things in which the country is less efficient and discourage the production of other things in which the country has a comparative advantage. The total value of production, so far as consumers are concerned, is less than it would otherwise be—and this means that real wages are held down by reason of tariffs. So, rather than *protecting* domestic wages generally, tariffs *lower* real wages in all countries affected.

That is all very well, you may say, but wouldn't a free trade policy lead to unemployment?

Do Tariffs Prevent Unemployment?

This argument is expressed in a number of ways. One is that the removal of a tariff, after an industry has become adjusted to it, will result in unemployment. Another is that by means of tariffs we can put our people to work making the things we now import and thus create employment. Today, there is fear in some quarters of a world-wide depression and unemployment. Some say: "We don't want such-and-such a country exporting its unemployment to us."

We have observed that if a tariff is removed, a protected industry may be forced out of business by foreign competition. If this happens, the workers in that industry will have to find employment elsewhere. In the embroidery illustration, it is not denied that the existence of the tariff permits some workers to be employed in embroidery manufacturing who would not otherwise be so employed. But what is often lost sight of is that many other job opportunities not now in existence would become available in this country if people could buy the imported embroidery and spend their tariff money as they please. The money which the consumer formerly had to pay for tariffs could be spent to purchase new products or to purchase more of existing products. This spending would automatically bring into existence new industries or increase the number of jobs available in established industries.

If the "disemployed" workers have mastered special skills, useful only in the discontinued industry, they may have to learn new ones. This argument, while often convincing, has been overstressed. Can you think of skills of this kind? It is true that the *short-run* adjustment may inconvenience those people who have to turn to new jobs. But everyone, including those same people, will benefit from the importation of a competing product at a lower price—thus permitting concentration on the production of things for which our methods are better suited.

The resulting unemployment should be only temporary and no more serious than the shift in employment going on constantly all over the country. The transfer of cotton mills from New England to the South caused a similar type of temporary unemployment. The failure of any business requires similar adjustments. If no business in America had ever been allowed to fail—if the government had always intervened—we would have had complete government ownership and control many, many years ago.

Tariffs turn a country toward self-sufficiency. A farm family might erect such a high tariff wall around its farm that there could be no trade in goods and services with outsiders. Certainly, no one would be unemployed on that farm, but neither would there be the high level of living the family now enjoys. If the tariff wall around the farm were removed, no one would necessarily be disemployed, and the farmer's household would enjoy a vastly higher level of living—and so would outsiders.

Prolonged unemployment among people who are willing and able to work is impossible in a thoroughly free market. The only reason for such a situation's existing— as it did from 1930 to 1940 in this country—is that labor, through controls of one type or another, prices itself out of the market, or employers, for a variety of reasons, decide to close shop rather than to offer work at the reduced wage rates they may be able to afford.

Therefore, the question of employment or unemployment, except for temporary adjustments, has no place in a consideration of tariffs. It would be as logical to argue that the buggy whip industry should have been subsidized in order to keep its workers employed when there no longer was a demand for buggy whips.

One might argue that the mistake was made in raising the tariff barrier in the first place; that the inconveniences caused by its removal would now be too great; and that we must continue to burden ourselves with this mistake. This, of course, is a political answer, not an economic one. This type of reasoning would halt all progress.

Do Tariffs Protect Our Level of Living?

Of all the arguments in support of tariffs, the one of their protecting our level of living should be the easiest to refute. As stated before, the level of living in a nation is determined by the amount of goods and services available and wanted for consumption.

People are more productive when they are free to specialize and to trade—when they are free to accumulate capital with which tools can be provided for the specialized workers.

The pattern of production within our own country is perhaps the best illustration of how free trade builds a higher level of living. Steel is produced in Pittsburgh, automobiles in Detroit, cotton in the South, meat and grain in the Midwest and the Great Plains, shoes in St. Louis, clothing in New England and New York—just to mention a few of the products and areas of specialization.

Take any one of these areas—say Wayne County, in which the city of Detroit is located—and build a tariff wall at its borders to shut off completely the flow of goods in and out of the county. What level of living would you then find in Wayne County? Well, to begin with, it is inconceivable that enough food could be grown in the county to support its present 2,500,000 people. The few who *could* live there would have to become practically self-sufficient—raising their own food, building their own homes, making their own clothing. There would be little time left to build automobiles, to study medicine, or to engage in other specialties.

"Yes," you may say, "but tariffs don't completely shut off trade." True, but they shut off trade to whatever extent they are effective. The effect of a tariff on wool is that we must employ more of our domestic resources in the production of wool than would be necessary if we imported it. A tariff on Swiss watches encourages the production of watches in our own country because it prevents their importation at a lower cost. And by keeping prices higher, such tariffs reduce our consumption of wool and watches.

We could raise a tariff barrier against the importation of bananas. If it were high enough, producers in this country would, no doubt, find it possible to grow a few bananas under glass to sell at very high prices to a small market. The level of living, so far as bananas contribute to it, would be decidedly reduced. What would happen, in this case, is that consumers would turn to other fruits; they would be denied the freedom of choice which they now enjoy. The workers drawn into banana production would be taken from other occupations more naturally suited to this country—more productive by the measure of a free market. And everyone's level of living would be reduced.

The American Indians

A high degree of self-sufficiency is possible, of course. The American Indians approached it; the early American settlers practiced it of necessity. But the level of living at that time was very low. Before the White Man came, the area that is now the United States supported fewer than 1,000,000 American Indians—and in a very meager fashion, despite the vast stores of natural resources. Some may argue that self-sufficiency is a more satisfying way of life than we now enjoy; that, however, is not an economic question, and it is outside the scope of this discussion.

Free exchange—whether between individuals, villages, states, or nations—makes for a higher level of living. Tariffs and other trade restrictions force people toward self-sufficiency and result in a lower level of living.

Tariffs Lower Level of Living

Bastiat tells a little story which illustrates how tariffs lower the level of living:

"A poor vine-dresser of the Gironde had trained with fond enthusiasm a slip of vine, which, after much fatigue and much labour, yielded him at length a tun of wine; . . . 'I shall sell it,' said he to his wife, 'and with the price I shall buy stuff sufficient to enable you to furnish a trousseau for our daughter.' The honest countryman repaired to the nearest town, and met a Belgian and an Englishman. The Belgian said to him: 'Give me your cask of wine, and I will give you in exchange fifteen parcels of stuff.' The Englishman said: 'Give me your wine, and I will give you twenty parcels of stuff; for we English can manufacture the stuff cheaper than the Belgians.' But a Customhouse officer, who was present interposed, and said: 'My good friend, exchange with the Belgian if you think proper, but my orders are to prevent you from making an exchange with the Englishman.' 'What!' exclaimed the countryman; 'you wish me to be content with fifteen parcels of stuff which have come from Brussels when I can get twenty parcels which have come from Manchester?' 'Certainly; don't you see that France would be a loser if you received twenty parcels instead of fifteen?' 'I am at a loss to understand you,' said the vine-dresser. 'And I am at a loss to explain it,' rejoined the Customhouse official; 'but the thing is certain, for all our deputies, ministers, and journalists agree in this, that the more a nation receives in exchange for a given quantity of its products, the more it is impoverished.' The peasant found it necessary to conclude a bargain with the Belgian. The daughter of the peasant got only three-quarters of her trousseau; and these simple people are still asking themselves how it happens that one is ruined by receiving four instead of three; and why a person is richer with three dozens of towels than with four dozens."

Tariffs and Infant Industries

Another argument for tariffs is that new industries cannot survive if they must compete with firmly established industries in other countries—"Give them a chance to get established, and then they can compete."

History has shown that protection in the form of tariffs imposed for this reason is difficult, if not impossible, to throw off. The protected infant never grows up to attain self-responsibility. And little wonder! In any industry, protected or not, there are firms which are barely able to stay in business—even though other firms in the same industry are operated profitably. If the crutch of tariffs is removed, these marginal producers must either improve their efficiency or go out of business. If they can do the former, why didn't they do it before the crutch was removed?

Who is to say that a prospective new industry will eventually become a successful one? Government ofcials?—or businessmen who know something about the industry? Businessmen are accustomed to taking risks; and the capital will be found to finance a business through its formative years if its prospects appear promising enough.

Confusion of Means and Ends

Those who use the infant-industry argument appear to place emphasis on the virtue of industry, as such, rather than on the goods produced. They seem to be confusing means and ends. We must not lose sight of the fact that *consumption is the sole end and purpose of all production.*

Business firms are constantly experimenting with new products and new methods of production. Some are successful; many are failures. What reason is there to ask a government employee to substitute his judgment, backed by the taxpayer's money, for the producer's judgment, backed by his own money?

Is an "infant industry" any different in principle from a new firm coming into a field already established? Suppose a new firm is formed to produce automobiles. "Give it a chance to get established and then it can compete." The "infant industry" argument would demand that such a firm be subsidized with government money until it reaches adolescence. How much progress would this country have made under such a policy?

India and China

And finally, if the infant-industry argument has any validity at all, this country, of all nations, would seem to be the last one to need it. Any usefulness of this procedure would seem to be in countries like India and China where industry is weak or nonexistent. Why don't the Chinese have a tariff to exclude our automobiles and radios until such time as they develop their own industries and can manufacture these products?

In a roundabout way, we are partially doing this for various countries through some of our give-away foreign aid schemes. We give the "backward" nations money that is often used as a subsidy to make up the difference between their costs of production and ours. Our gifts often encourage them to continue some inefficient or questionable production. In some respects, the receiving nations regard this in the same way they regard the idea of imposing a tariff against our goods to equalize this difference—"It is only fair." And some of us have added to the general confusion by accepting the fallacious idea that we would suffer a depression at home if we stopped giving away our products abroad.

Another illustration of the inconsistencies which arise when governments try to "do something" for other nations is found in the conflict between our foreign aid program and our tariff policy. On the one hand, we give vast sums of money to a nation to help it "get on its feet" and produce for export—to alleviate its "dollar shortage." On the other hand, we raise barriers in the form of tariffs and other trade restrictions to prevent the importation of their products to our country.

Loans by individuals or firms in this country to foreign industries are an entirely different matter. In such cases, individuals may appraise the risks they wish to take with their own money. And all this, of course, has nothing to do with private charitable gifts which American citizens may wish to make to people of foreign nations.

Tariffs and National Self-Sufficiency

It will readily be recognized that the topics under which tariffs are here being discussed are not entirely exclusive of one another and overlap to a considerable extent. The argument for self-sufficiency is closely allied to the level-of-living argument, and it will also be discussed later as an important part of the national defense argument.

National self-sufficiency is sometimes expressed as "economic nationalism," "isolationism," or the "keep the money at home" idea. The argument is that we would be better off, as a nation, if we did not trade with other nations. We would develop our own resources more fully; we would encourage domestic employment; and we would not become dependent on other nations for goods and services.

On the question of dependency, it should be recalled again that trade is a two-way project. For example, if we gear our industry to the use of imported lead, we are, of course, dependent on foreign production of lead. But the foreign producer is just as dependent on our market for whatever he receives in trade for his lead. It is not a one-way street.

One might as well argue that the automobile worker in Detroit should not be dependent on the farmer for his food, nor the farmer dependent on the Detroit worker for his automobile. The farmer is as dependent on the automobile worker for his market as the automobile worker is dependent on the farmer for food. It is as logical to argue self-sufficiency for an individual as for a nation. As a matter of fact, the type of dependence engendered by free trade between individuals is a wholesome thing. So long as it is voluntary trade, friendships develop. Such trade is not a battle between opposing forces, as is sometimes claimed. Witness the friendships between the customers and the tradespeople in a small community.

We have already seen that a farmer, or a small group of people, may approach self-sufficiency, though at a very low level of living. But self-sufficiency is incompatible with technology, division of labor, and specialization in modern society.

It is possible for a nation to follow a "keep the money at home" policy, but the level of living of the nation will suffer as a consequence of thus rejecting opportunities. The principle of comparative advantage cannot be wished away by means of international trade barriers.

Few areas are as favorably adapted as the United States to a relatively high degree of self-subsistence. We have the agricultural resources to support a large population. In addition, we have iron, coal, oil, and other resources with which to develop our industries. But still we feel we must buy industrial diamonds, tin, tungsten, and many other products not found here.

The Contrast with England

Contrast our situation with that of England. Her agriculture would support only a relatively few million people if they were to be as well fed as we are in the United States. England has coal but had to import the raw materials to develop the great industry she possessed in the 19th century. It was no accident that, until the first World War, industrial Britain rose to great heights under free trade; and her decline over the past third of a century has been due in no small part to her renouncing free trade. Only recently, an observer in London wrote:

"There is one thing which can be done. London can do it. London can forget the statesmen and the politicians for a while; we can recognise the needs of men of every race and creed to exchange their goods or services one with another. We can offer again the great free exchange market.

"*Make London a Free Port, if you will*. London will

then have offered the world a policy which knows no colour bar; speaks all languages; creates wealth and does not destroy it. It is the one great peace offer which England can make *alone;* regardless of the policies of any other nation on earth."*

It is not a question of whether or not self-subsistence is possible. There are hermits who associate with the outside world to a limited degree only. There are small groups of individuals living secluded lives. There are even nations which are practically self-contained. In general, the larger the area, the more nearly possible it is to have a satisfactory self-subsistence economy. All people on this earth, as a group, are self-subsisting insofar as contact with the inhabitants of other planets is concerned. A large section of the earth—the Western Hemisphere or all of Europe or all of Asia—*could* be self-subsisting at a fairly high level. But for what purpose? What is lost by trade between individuals of different countries? Nothing; and the gains are obvious.

Economic nationalism is more likely to be a product of trade controlled by governments than of trade left to free individuals seeking profitable exchange wherever they may find it.

Tariffs and Dumping

The term *dumping* carries a fairly definite impression to most people, but to define it is not easy. When goods from one country are sold in another at prices below the

---

*The London Newsletter, V. R. Kimmitt, Editor, May, 1952, p. 4.

cost of producing them, the process is commonly called dumping. Presumably it doesn't matter whether it is an individual or a firm or a government that does it; it is still called dumping.

The argument against dumping is that domestic producers cannot meet "unfair" competition from abroad. The remedy often suggested is to raise a tariff wall against these products by an amount equal to the difference between what foreign producers are willing to sell for and their costs of production. Sometimes the comparison is even made with *our* costs of production.

Since when has the cost of production been the determining factor of the selling price? This idea is based on the labor theory of value, rather than on the market theory. Using this same argument, local tariffs should be levied against all domestic businesses which, for any reason, offer their products for sale at a price below the cost of production. Of course, the advocates of this argument demand that the government be given the power to determine the "true" cost of production. And don't laugh this off as a joke because it has been seriously proposed more than once. The proposal may be in the form of a subsidy rather than a tariff, but the reasoning is the same.

Losses and Dumping

Every year, many farmers produce something at a loss. Their cost of production is above their selling price; they are dumping their products on the market. The same is true of many grocery stores, hardware stores—in fact, can you think of a single type of business in which a few companies are not operating at a loss each year? By these standards, they are dumping their products and are indulging in "unfair" competition with businesses which are able to operate profitably.

If trading across national boundaries were carried on by individuals, the question of dumping would seldom arise. If a British woolen manufacturer, for example, offered to sell woolens to an American importer at a price below his cost of production, the American importer would, if he gave it any thought, merely think of it as his good fortune.

But if the British government bought up British woolens and sold them in this country at prices which our manufacturers thought were below the British production costs, an international incident would arise. Not that it is possible to *know* the costs of production in Britain or anywhere else; they differ from mill to mill.

Domestic Dumping

Dumping is a process that goes on domestically all the time, and it will occur in trade between nations as long as there is trade. When dumping involves only individual producers, we can be sure that it can't last long; the producer will soon have to change his ways or go out of business. While it lasts, it works to the advantage of the consumer, and he may as well get what benefits he can from it at the expense of the producer who chooses

58

to use up his resources in that way. Charity is a form of dumping in that the donor disposes of his property at less than his "cost of production." Should charity be prohibited?

Dried Eggs and Dumping

One of the clearest illustrations of dumping is the recent dried egg deal of our own government. The government bought huge quantities of eggs at high prices in order to support the egg market in this country. The eggs were dried and stored for some time in a Kansas cave. Eventually the government, feeling that it had to get rid of the dried eggs, dumped them (or gave them away) on world markets and at home at prices far below the government's cost of production—purchase price, processing, storage, etc.

Actually, dumping is more a fear and an illusion than an actuality. Steel producers, for example, may fear that some hostile foreign power may dump steel into America for a long enough period to cause some of our steel companies to fail or go out of business, thus withering away some of our productive capacity. This is merely a theoretical argument based on a groundless fear. Should some foreign power attempt to do this, it would seem a simple solution for American steel companies or steel users to buy up all the steel offered at the low prices, keeping their own plants in a stand-by condition until the foreign source of supply is exhausted or the dumpers go broke.

Finally, once the theory of imposing tariffs to prevent

dumping is adopted, what is to prevent its being used every time a foreign product can be sold in this country at a price below that for which our producers can manufacture and sell it?

Dumping is not unlike "price cutting" and "loss leaders," as used domestically. Any attempt to prevent these practices by law is an invasion of private property rights; it will lead to a pyramiding of controls, which in turn must lead to a strait-jacketing of industry and commerce. When that happens, freedom will be only a theory to read about in the history books.

Helping Backward Areas

Much has been said in recent years about helping backward areas of the world. There are backward areas in the United States; there are backward states, backward counties, backward communities—yes, and backward individuals within each community. Variation is a law of nature; so long as there are individuals, some will be better off than others. Some will seem to be backward in the eyes of others. But to talk about it is futile.

One might raise the question of what the effect would be on world friendship and good will to speak in such terms about other nations. Suppose your neighbor spoke of you as a backward person!

Can there be any doubt that the best way to help another individual—or another nation—is to let him help himself? Hire him, if you will, or buy his product so that he may learn to work, produce, and trade.

Freedom of opportunity to work, to own, and to trade offers perhaps the best-known self-help to economic improvement. In the United States, the phenomenal rise to our present high level of living has been due in no small part to there having been few, if any, economic barriers at state lines or elsewhere within the country. We have demonstrated what free trade and a relatively free market can do for an economy. True, there are areas here which might be called "backward" if their average level of living were compared with other areas in the United States; but, if transplanted to other places in the world, these areas would stand out as anything but backward.

The redeeming feature in opening our markets to free trade among the so-called "backward" countries of the world is that it would cost us nothing to do so. On net balance, we would gain as much as they. Here is an opportunity to demonstrate to the world that when we glibly talk "free enterprise" we talk it with conviction—not with restriction.

The elimination of all trade barriers would have three very important beneficial effects:

1. It would permit our economy to gain from the specialization and comparative advantage in production to be found all over the world.

2. It would help the so-called underdeveloped areas of the world to help themselves. It would give them a better chance to produce and trade.

3. It would be the best way to cement friendly relations between Americans and other peoples all

61

over the world. How can one individual become angry with another when they are permitted to trade freely and voluntarily, knowing that both parties to the deal will benefit? In such trade, there is no danger of secret diplomacy, of playing special favorites, of handling other nations as pawns—pitting one against the other to seek a gain or even to attempt a precarious balance.

Tariffs and Conservation of Resources

It is sometimes argued that since a nation's natural resources are limited, they should be exported, if at all, in limited quantities. Tariffs are proposed as a way of limiting the import of goods which might be exchanged for such exports. Other means of restricting exports are also advocated.

It is clear that the natural resources of a nation may be depleted through international give-away schemes and wars. But in ordinary peacetime trade carried on between individuals and firms of different nations, no such charge can be made with regard to overall resources. As I have repeatedly pointed out, *a voluntary trade benefits both parties*. If a firm in the United States exports copper, there is, of course, less copper in this country. But whatever this firm receives for the copper is more valuable to the firm than is the copper. And, presumably, no domestic buyer of copper is willing to pay more than the foreign buyer; otherwise the copper would not go for export. To that extent, because someone gains and no one loses, consumers are better off after the trade. Such is the case with all voluntary exchanges.

"Yes," you may say, "but copper is a scarce material, and we should conserve it." Every economic good is scarce; otherwise it would command no price. If it were to become scarce enough and valuable enough, the domestic consumers would probably bid the price up to a point where no foreign buyer could afford it.

It may be argued that mere men, acting individually, cannot know the future needs of mankind and, therefore, cannot be wise enough to conserve scarce materials. So a bureau or commission made up of these men is established by government to make such decisions!

In connection with conservation, it has been repeatedly demonstrated that no one is more concerned with the conservation and use of property than its owner. No better system of conservation has ever been discovered than private ownership. What the government owns belongs to no one, and the likelihood of its wise conservation is remote indeed. This is as true of products for export as it is of those traded and used domestically.

Tariffs and National Defense

Bastiat is reported to have said that if goods do not cross frontiers, armies will.

The cause of war is a hotly debated question which probably will never be settled to everyone's satisfaction. Nevertheless, there appears to be considerable evidence to show that wars are fought for economic as well as political reasons—restrictions against trade, monopoly control of raw materials, attempts to be "self-contained," isolationism, nationalism, and the like. Many persons believe that the best single deterrent to war would be a willingness on the part of individuals the world over to trade freely.

With this thought in mind, the removal of tariffs and other trade restrictions should be a prime weapon of national defense. But instead, the national defense argument is often used to advance the restriction idea, which, as Bastiat said, promotes war.

It is asked what we would do in case of war if we were placed at the mercy of foreign countries for essential products. Bastiat answered that question in this way:

"The kind of dependence which results from exchange, from commercial transactions, is a reciprocal dependence. We cannot be dependent on the foreigner without the foreigner being dependent on us. . . . To break up natural relations is not to place ourselves in a state of independence, but in a state of isolation. . . . A nation isolates itself looking forward to the possibility of war; but is not this very act of isolating itself the beginning of war? . . . Let countries be permanent markets for each other's produce; let their reciprocal relations be such that they cannot be broken without inflicting on each other the double suffering of privation and a glut of commodities; and they will no longer stand in need of naval armaments, which ruin them, and overgrown armies, which crush them; . . . and war will disappear for want of what supports it, for want of resources, inducements, pretexts, and popular sympathy."

It is not proposed to discuss here the logistics of war —to debate how best to prosecute a war or prepare for a war. The intent of this discussion is merely to point out one thing which leads to war and some of the pitfalls of trade restrictions under the guise of wartime measures.

Peanuts for Defense

Section 104 of the Defense Production Act of 1952 restricts the importation of peanuts, among other products, " . . . for the protection of the essential security interests and economy of the United States in the existing emergency in international relations. . . ." While one might readily concede that there is an "existing emergency in international relations," one might seriously question whether a restriction on the importation of peanuts would alleviate or aggravate such an emergency.

We find a trade association of the American leather glove industry offering this argument for high tariffs:

"Warm gloves, properly made, are indispensable in cold climates. The soldier, sailor or aviator who suffers the loss of his hands becomes, at once, a helpless liability. . . . To turn out the millions of gloves necessary to protect our service forces requires a healthy glove industry within our own borders. We must, therefore, be cautious, in the interests of national defense, when doing anything which would tend to destroy a United States industry and leave us dependent upon foreign producers in time of war."

The spokesman for another industry—one in which a large amount of highly skilled hand labor is involved and which finds it increasingly difficult to compete with foreign producers—says that the skills of their workers are highly useful in time of war, and high tariffs are necessary to insure the industry's survival in this country in anticipation of such an emergency.

These illustrations are typical of industries which are faced with competition from foreign products and which seek special favors—under the guise of national defense—at the expense of consumers generally. In granting such special favors, we lose sight of the fact that consumption is the sole end and purpose of all production, and we place the emphasis on the industry as such.

Once the door is opened to the granting of special favors, there is no logical point at which to stop. What industry is *not,* in this same sense, essential to national defense? In two global wars, we have discovered that more than men and guns and tanks and planes are essential. Yes, even peanuts!

If such reasoning is followed, the logical end is to close our borders to the importation of everything. And this means closing them to the exportation of everything.

Productive Capacity

The fact of the matter is that, more often than not, a war is started with little or no idea as to what weapons will be used before the war's end. Political leaders, usually lacking in business experience, do not seem to understand that a major war is primarily a test of the productive capacity of the respective contestants. They try to stockpile war goods and withhold military supplies from the enemy. They frequently act as though the goods on hand when the war starts were all that each side would ever have. They underestimate the power of resistance and the capacity for production of a relatively free people who are not subject to absolute governmental control.

With increasing governmental control, our own political leaders are tending more·and more in that same fallacious direction as the years go by. At the beginning of World War II, the government began to worry about our supply of natural rubber. It ordered American industry to build factories and produce synthetic rubber, regardless of the cost as compared with the cost of natural rubber. True, this synthetic rubber was needed to fight the war. But what is not generally recognized is that American private industry—individuals—had experimented and learned how to produce synthetic rubber at least 18 months before Pearl Harbor. All that the government actually accomplished was to declare war. The people, as always, had to produce the tools of war and furnish the manpower to use them. We should always remember that the government can only *withhold* ideas and information and materials from its citizenry; it cannot *give* them anything beyond what they themselves are capable of producing.

As a war measure, a government is inclined to stop

the international flow of information and goods and services, in the belief that this is a way of injuring the actual or potential enemy. But the greater injury, more dangerous because it is unseen, is to the productive capacity of the workers of the country. To stop their voluntary trading is to deprive them of the gains from such trade—gains which may be greater than any advantages that might have accrued to the enemy nation.

Let the Enemy Pay

If American citizens were allowed to conduct themselves according to sound economic principles rather than political controls, a startling thing would happen. People of other nations, instead of the American taxpayers, would be paying for our current preparedness program. The cost of our war plants and experimentation in the development of war tools would be financed by sales of war materials—planes, guns, tanks, and other weapons—to our potential enemies. We can produce these things more efficiently than they, for we have the capital and the skill. And if our potential enemies could be induced to become dependent upon us for their armaments, they could easily be defeated if they were ever so stupid as to declare war on us. Since they would have developed no armament factories of their own, they would be doomed as soon as their stockpiles were exhausted or became obsolete. Would any people be so misguided as to attempt to destroy the source of their supplies?

In return for our armaments, potential enemy nations would have to offer us something more valuable than these war goods. Of course, such a plan of free trade does not conform to traditional military strategy. It isn't "practical" from a military point of view—you can't start a war by means of free trade. Military strategy deals with the subject of war; sound economics calls for peaceful trade. Until the people themselves recognize that these ideas are hopelessly opposed to each other, political and military strategists will keep right on leading nations into wars.

Our fear of being cut off from sources of essential materials during times of war has been more a theory than a fact. The market has a way of being supplied, even though drastic attempts are made to prevent it. Experience with so-called black markets has demonstrated this. At times, we have attempted to keep our exports out of the hands of "enemy" countries, only to find out later that, by devious and roundabout exchanges, they reached there anyway. It is common practice for warring nations to trade with each other—by indirect means, through agents in neutral countries.

There seems to be ample evidence that, even for national defense, tariffs have no place in our economy. First, and most important, free trade between individuals of different nations contributes to the friendship and good feelings which are conducive to peace. Trade restrictions, on the other hand, lead to hatred, conniving, jealousy—incidents which in turn may lead to conflict. Secondly, tariffs or trade restrictions weaken a nation's economy and make it less able to withstand attacks, should they come.

Much concern is expressed over European unity. For decades, attempts have been made to unite the countries of Europe by political alliances, international cartels, and trade agreements of all sorts. Actually, the elimination of trade barriers between European nations and the restoration of trade opportunities to individuals and firms would go further toward bringing about a peaceful Europe than would any other scheme that could be devised. And this could be accomplished without the least disturbance of political, religious, or other cultural institutions.

What to Do about Tariffs

The author has neither the desire nor the ability to present here a detailed blueprint for the elimination of trade restrictions in this country or throughout the world. He is convinced that once there is a will to remove these restrictions, there will somehow be a way.

The will to remove restrictions on trade can come about only through understanding—through the realization that restrictions do not yield the benefits claimed for them. Worse than that, they are harmful—harmful economically and harmful to the cause of peace, friendship, and good will, at home and abroad.

On the surface, tariff protection seems to offer benefits to the owners and workers of a protected industry. When a tariff is first applied, the producers of the particular product affected have a price advantage which should be reflected in higher profits. But tariffs do not prohibit domestic competition within an industry. The higher profits attract newcomers to the field, and competition tends to erase the gains from the special privilege. After this happens, the producers are back in their former competitive position. In order to maintain any benefit, they will have to continue to ask for new privileges as the old ones lose their power—much as a drug addict must use more and more of the drug to avoid the suffering it is supposed to relieve.

Thus, the so-called "benefits" of tariff protection are illusory—the only consequence of the tariff being that the domestic owners and workers are competing with one another in an industry erected on a false base. The base is false and weak because it is supported by the threat of force—force which directs individual spending —instead of by voluntary choice. The force is directed against consumers, the friends and neighbors of those who seek special privileges for themselves. But consumers do not respond kindly to force or threats of force. They have only so much buying power, and they cannot be forced to buy more of everything. Nor will they buy a commodity as freely as before if its price is forced upward by a "protective" tariff. Thus, tariffs serve merely to put the whole economy on an artificial foundation instead of on a sound business foundation. No one really gains—and nearly everyone loses—by this arrangement. It stifles progress.

Adjustments such as those which would be required

by the removal of tariffs are taking place constantly in a free economy. When the automobile made its appearance, the operators of livery stables and the manufacturers of buggies were inconvenienced. They had to turn to something else. But they soon found themselves benefiting in two ways: First, as consumers, they benefited generally from the automobile; and second, the new job opportunities within the new and expanding automobile industry were more attractive than their old jobs in a dying industry. Thus, the removal of trade restrictions would not be as painful as it may at first appear—even to those who think they benefit from them.

An Invalid Argument

To argue that tariffs cannot be removed when an industry or a nation has become adjusted to operating under trade restrictions is no different in principle than to argue against all technological change and advance.

It is claimed that a removal of tariffs will harm the capitalists who have invested in the production of the protected item—also, that it will harm the workers who have developed special skills. These are, at most, short-run effects and tend to be overmagnified. Advocating tariffs on these grounds is the same as advocating subsidies to protect candlemakers from the competition of electricity.

Such arguments indicate, however, that it is politically difficult to remove restrictions once they have become established. Powerful minority interests vigorously withstand changes of this type. "Tariffs should be removed gradually," say some, "in order not to offend too severely those who have a direct interest in the protected industry." This overlooks the persons who have long been offended by not being able to exchange to advantage. It argues that the offense to the consumer may be continued without injustices.

A familiar argument is: "We are willing to give up our protection if all others will give up theirs." As a political argument, this is fairly effective since it is practically impossible to face the combined forces of all minority groups. Economically, of course, the argument has no validity. The way to begin is to begin. The amount of human energy released by the removal of restrictions will be astounding.

The Plea for Exceptions

Perhaps the greatest obstacle to the removal of trade barriers is the belief expressed by small groups of producers: "Yes, but our case is different; an exception should be granted in just this one instance." Grant a single exception, and the floodgates are opened to all sorts of pressure groups. The result will be a continuation of the political chaos which we now find in the area of trade restrictions.

The long-run benefits of free trade so far outweigh the short-run inconveniences to the protected groups that it is inconceivable that sufficient understanding to bring about free trade will not someday be achieved.

Summary and Conclusions

Basically, the issue of tariffs and other trade restrictions is a moral one. This is not to deny that it is also an economic issue. It is merely a matter of emphasis. Unless economic principles are in harmony with good moral principles, they are not good economics.

Government grows strong and dictatorial by the granting of special favors. Trade restrictions are just another of the handouts which a government can grant, thereby increasing its power over individuals—to the detriment of all.

The point of view set forth in this discussion argues neither for nationalism (isolationism) nor for internationalism. Both of these terms imply a kind of design by government. And both, when implemented by governmental design — force — have very serious consequences. Instead of aiming for either of these objectives, we would argue merely to allow individuals to trade freely with one another, when and where they wish—with a minimum of governmental interference.

The moral basis for free trade rests on the assumption that an individual has the right to the product of his own labor—stealing is bad because ownership is good. This involves property rights. Property rights are human rights, and to try to distinguish between them is merely to play with words—and on emotions.*

---

*For a more complete discussion of this subject, see: Paul L. Poirot, *Property Rights and Human Rights* (Irvington-on-Hudson, N. Y.: Foundation for Economic Education, Inc., 1952).

The right to own property involves the right to use it, to keep it, to give it away, or to exchange it. Unless this is possible, one does not own property. To lay obstacles in the path of ownership, use, or exchange of property is a violation of the human right to own property.

Economists from Adam Smith down to the present have quite generally agreed that tariffs are bad economics. And it is not difficult to discover why:

1. *Tariffs and other trade restrictions contribute to scarcity rather than to abundance.* We are sometimes fooled by the introduction of money into trade; but basically, it is the abundance of goods and services, widely distributed, that contributes to a high level of material well-being. A person who offers money in a trade is generally thought to be a buyer or consumer. But how does one acquire the money in the first place except by producing something for sale? Each one has something to offer in exchange for what he wants. Why is one party the seller any more than the other?

2. *A voluntary exchange of goods or services between two individuals results in a benefit to each party.* To say that only the seller benefits is a fallacy. Why is it so commonly believed that you confer a favor upon a person by buying what he offers you? When you offer your money to a grocery clerk for a purchase, he usually says, "Thank you!" Why isn't it just as appropriate for the customer to say, "Thank you!" for the services rendered by the store?

3. *There is ample evidence that a high level of living in any country cannot be achieved without a high degree*

of division of labor—specialization. Instead of a person's being a "jack of all trades," he is the master of one. This calls for a high degree of co-operative effort and exchange. Production by this process rests on the principle of comparative advantage—of production where conditions are most favorable. Ludwig von Mises, in his book, *Human Action,* says:

"All that a tariff can achieve is to divert production from those locations in which the output per unit of input is higher to locations in which it is lower. It does not increase production; it curtails it. . . .

"Government does not have the power to encourage one branch of production except by curtailing other branches. It withdraws the factors of production from those branches in which the unhampered market would employ them and directs them into other branches. . . . It may subsidize openly or disguise the subsidy in enacting tariffs and thus forcing its subjects to defray the costs. . . .

"While government has no power to make people more prosperous by interference with business, it certainly does have the power to make them less satisfied by restriction of production."*

4. *A fallacy of protectionists is that employment, of itself, is a worthy economic objective. Employment, however, is merely a means to an end—and the end is production for consumption.* No doubt, employment was high during the building of the Great Wall of China or

*Ludwig von Mises, *Human Action* (New Haven: Yale University Press, 1949), p. 737.

the Pyramids of Egypt. A dictator can always achieve full employment. Hitler did it in Germany, and we had our leaf-raking projects.

But under freedom—freedom to produce and to trade voluntarily—men will have just as much employment as they desire. Actually, tariffs have nothing to do with employment. Employment can be high or low—with or without such trade restrictions. Tariffs do not create better jobs for individuals. They simply tend to keep people working at jobs which are less productive of useful goods and services than they would be under free trade.

5. *Protectionists have claimed that wage levels can be maintained or increased by shutting out imports from areas with low real wages.* Wage levels are determined by the productivity of labor. This, in turn, is determined by the investment of capital in the tools of production.

Advantage to Both Countries

The exportation of American products to China—a nation of low real wages—and our importation of Chinese products raise real wages in both countries. The products we import are more valuable to us than our exports; otherwise the trade would not be made. Rather than produce the imported product here, our own labor is released to produce something we are better fitted to produce.

6. *Failure to recognize that satisfaction of desires is the sole purpose and end of production has led protec-*

77

tionists to support tariffs, subsidies, and other measures.
Had we consistently failed in this recognition, we would
now be subsidizing 80 per cent of our population in
agricultural pursuits, as well as in the manufacture of
buggy whips and candles. Economic progress cannot
take place under such a system.

The removal of tariffs restores justice to consumers—
to millions and millions of consumers. The fact that it
may seem to result in a temporary inconvenience for a
few producers is merely the correction of an injustice
previously established.

Tariffs and World Peace

Aside from their many economic disadvantages, trade
restrictions are most devastating in their effect on the
relations between nations.

In an address in New York on June 9, 1952, Sir Miles
Thomas, Chairman of the British Overseas Airways Cor-
poration, said that some British manufacturers were dis-
turbed by the tendency of some United States manufacturers of competitive or related items to seek home
protection against foreign competition. He went on to say:

"The very essence of our being, the very survival
of the free nations of the world—must depend upon
a two-way flow of goods and services. If you place
a brake on that you inevitably discriminate against
your own future as well as ours. Forgive me if I so
far forget myself as your guest . . . if I ask you whether
you prefer to have the dollars supplied by an already

over-loaded taxpayer or by a satisfied consumer? . . .

"Surely it is by the reduction rather than the increase of international trade barriers that the cause of peace can best be preserved."*

Trading, when engaged in by individuals, is a peaceful, friendly project. When controlled by governments, it provides opportunity for favoritism, intrigue, and a display of power politics. It cannot lead to other than animosity, suspicion, and unfriendly relations.

We pretend, on the one hand, to favor a united, friendly Europe. But at the same time, we encourage trade restrictions and controls of all sorts. For example, we promote in Europe a government controlled and operated cartel for certain basic industries. Chaos and strife are certain to result, whereas the promotion of free trade between individuals and firms of all nations would go far toward bringing about the peace we seek.

In his recent book, *The Trade of Nations,* Michael A. Heilperin said:

"It is the thesis of this book that world trade based on the operations of free markets and on the personal enterprise of free men fosters the cause of international understanding, while trade straitjacketed by governmental controls and subject to authoritarian dictation from the top becomes a servant of nationalism and an abundant source of ill will, friction, and conflict."†

New York Times, June 10, 1952.
†Michael A. Heilperin, *The Trade of Nations* (New York: Alfred A. Knopf, 1952), pp. iv-v.

Free trade is such a simple solution for so many of the world's ills. It doesn't require endless hours of debate in the United Nations, or the International Labor Organization, or the Food and Agriculture Organization, or any other worldwide debating society. It requires only that *one nation* see the light and remove *its* restrictions. The results will be immediate and widespread.

It isn't necessary for all nations to agree jointly and simultaneously to remove restrictions. If only one nation does it, some good is accomplished—both for itself and for its customers. A great nation, such as the United States, could do it and thus set an example for others to follow. It would not be meddling in the affairs of other nations; it would merely be looking after the best interests of its own citizens. And instead of being resentful, other nations would be eternally grateful.

If goods do not cross frontiers, armies will!

"If, to please the people, we offer what we ourselves disapprove, how can we afterwards defend our work? Let us raise a standard to which the wise and honest can repair. The event is in the hand of God."

Attributed to George Washington
during the Constitutional Convention

Index

About the Publisher

The Foundation for Economic Education (FEE) is a "home" for the friends of freedom everywhere. Its spirit is uplifting, reassuring, and contagious. FEE has inspired the creation of numerous similar organizations at home and abroad.

FEE is the oldest conservative research organization dedicated to the preservation of individual freedom and the private property order. It was established in 1946 by Chamber of Commerce executive Leonard E. Read, and guided by its advisor, the eminent Austrian economist Ludwig von Mises.

The Foundation publishes *The Freeman*, an award winning monthly journal. Every issue offers more than a dozen articles dealing with topics of interest from the broad fields of economics, history, and moral philosophy. *The Freeman* also features popular monthly columns by Lawrence Reed, Mark Skousen, and Doug Bandow. It is distributed free of charge to schools, colleges, seminaries, and libraries; individual donors of $30.00 or more ($45.00 for foreign donors) are added to the mailing list for FEE services.

The Foundation publishes books and booklets that affirm and expound the freedom philosophy. It carries an inventory of more than 400 titles and markets them wholesale and directly with its subscribers and readers.

FEE produces one book a month in its publishing program. The Freeman Classics series includes anthologies of the best essays and articles published throughout the years. In addition, the Foundation prints time-honored works by Leonard Read, Ludwig von Mises, Edmund Opitz, Frederic Bastiat, Henry Hazlitt, and others. It also commissions and publishes original works of philosophy, economics, and biography. A free catalogue is available upon request.

The Foundation conducts a wide variety of seminars. During the summer it offers one-week courses of adult education at the FEE site in Irvington-on-Hudson, New York. Each spring it sponsors weekend classes for undergraduates. Throughout the year, FEE hosts a popular series of Saturday evening Round-Table Discussions.

The Foundation supports an international network of Freeman Society Discussion Clubs which seek to improve the understanding of the first principles of a free and prosperous society. It encourages the formation of groups of any size and supports them with speakers and free literature.

Contributions to FEE are deductible from taxable income. Donations in any amount are welcome. For more information about deferred giving and charitable remainder trusts, please contact:

The Foundation for Economic Education
30 South Broadway
Irvington-on-Hudson, New York 10533
Phone: (914) 591-7230
Fax: (914) 591-8910
E-mail: freeman@westnet.com